SPECTRUM®
READERS

W9-AFU-923

LEVEL 1

CUTE!

Animal
Babies

By Teresa Domnauer

Carson-Dellosa
Publishing

SPECTRUM®

An imprint of Carson-Dellosa Publishing, LLC
P.O. Box 35665
Greensboro, NC 27425-5665

© 2014, Carson-Dellosa Publishing, LLC. Except as permitted under
the United States Copyright Act, no part of this publication may
be reproduced, stored, or distributed in any form or by any means
(mechanically, electronically, recording, etc.) without the prior written
consent of Carson-Dellosa Publishing, LLC. Spectrum is an imprint of
Carson-Dellosa Publishing, LLC.

carsondellosa.com

Printed in the USA. All rights reserved.
ISBN 978-1-4838-0110-0

01-002141120

Animal mothers take
care of their babies.
They feed their babies
to help them grow.
They teach their babies
how to survive.
They stay near their babies
to keep them safe.

Giraffe

A baby giraffe is
called a *calf*.
This mother snuggles
her baby.
The calf drinks milk from

Polar Bear

A baby polar bear is called a *cub*.
This mother protects her babies.
The cubs stay with their mother for four years or more.

Kangaroo

A baby kangaroo is called a *joey*. This mother carries her baby in her pouch. The joey stays in the pouch until it is ten months old.

Lion

A baby lion is called a *cub*.
This mother nuzzles her baby.
Lion cubs learn to hunt when they are one year old.

Zebra

A baby zebra is called a *colt*. This mother grazes with her baby. They live in family groups called *herds*.

14

Hippo

A baby hippo is called a *calf*. This mother swims with her baby. They stay cool in the water.

Leopard

A baby leopard is
called a *cub*.
This mother keeps her
babies safe.
Mothers teach their cubs
to hunt and play.

Gorilla

A baby gorilla is
called an *infant*.
This mother holds
her baby close.
Sometimes, infants ride
on their mothers' backs.

Elephant

A baby elephant is called a *calf*.
This mother drinks water with her baby.
They walk many miles to find water.

Koala

A baby koala is
called a *joey*.
This mother sleeps
in a tree with her baby.
They spend most of their
time high in the trees.

Harp Seal

A baby harp seal is called a *pup*. This mother keeps her baby on the ice. Harp seal pups have thick fur to keep them warm.

White-Tailed Deer

A baby deer is
called a *fawn*.
This mother licks
her baby.
The fawn will learn to
run away from danger.

Swan

A baby swan is
called a *cygnet*.
This mother teaches
her babies to swim.
Cygnets learn to swim
and run right after
they hatch.

Tiger

A baby tiger is
called a *cub*.
This mother rests
with her babies.
The cubs stay with their
mother until they learn
to hunt on their own.

CUTE! Animal Babies
Comprehension Questions

1. What is the name for a baby elephant?

2. How do kangaroo mothers carry their babies?

3. Why do hippo mothers and babies spend time in the water?

4. What do cygnets learn to do right after they hatch?

5. Why do harp seal pups have thick fur?

6. What is the name for a baby gorilla?

7. What do leopard cubs learn from their mothers? What do you learn from your parent?

8. What is the name for a zebra family group?

9. Where do mother and baby koalas spend most of their time?